ISBN 978-1-4803-4233-0

HAL•LEONARD®
CORPORATION
7777 W. BLUEMOUND RD. P.O. BOX 13819 MILWAUKEE, WI 53213

Visit Hal Leonard Online at
www.halleonard.com

CONTENTS

Blackbird

Words and Music by John Lennon and Paul McCartney

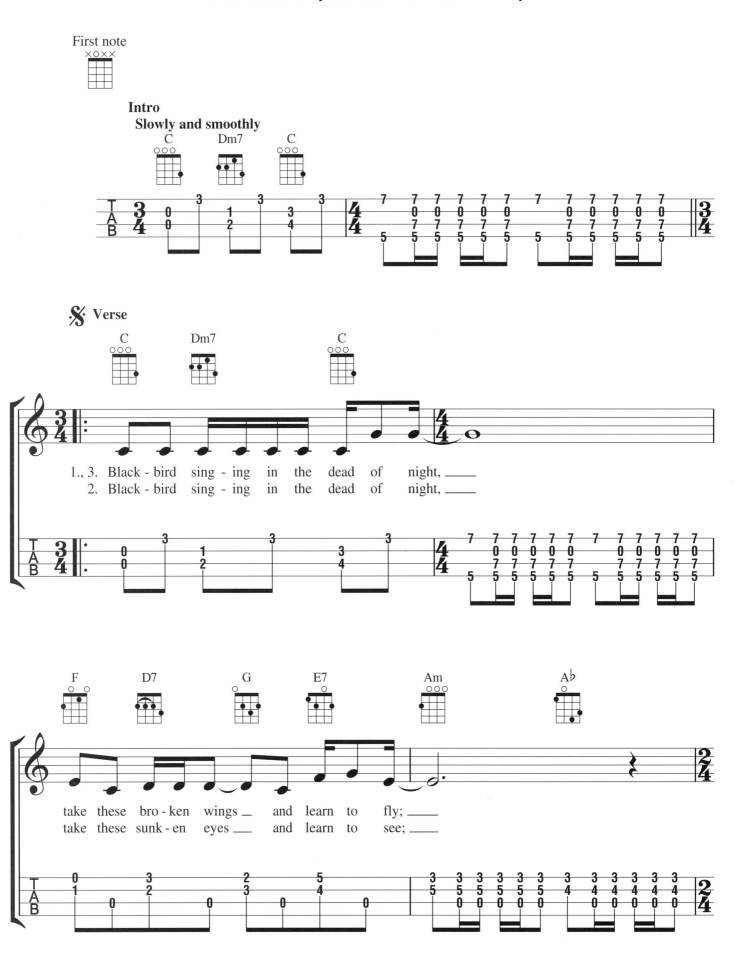

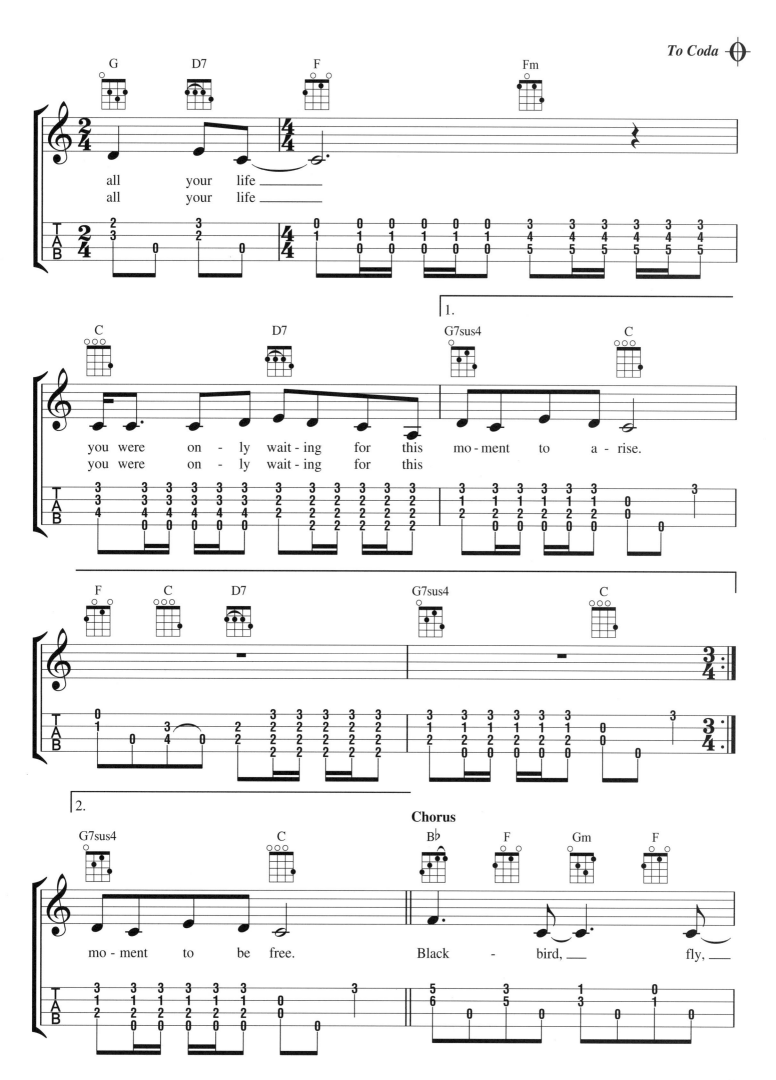

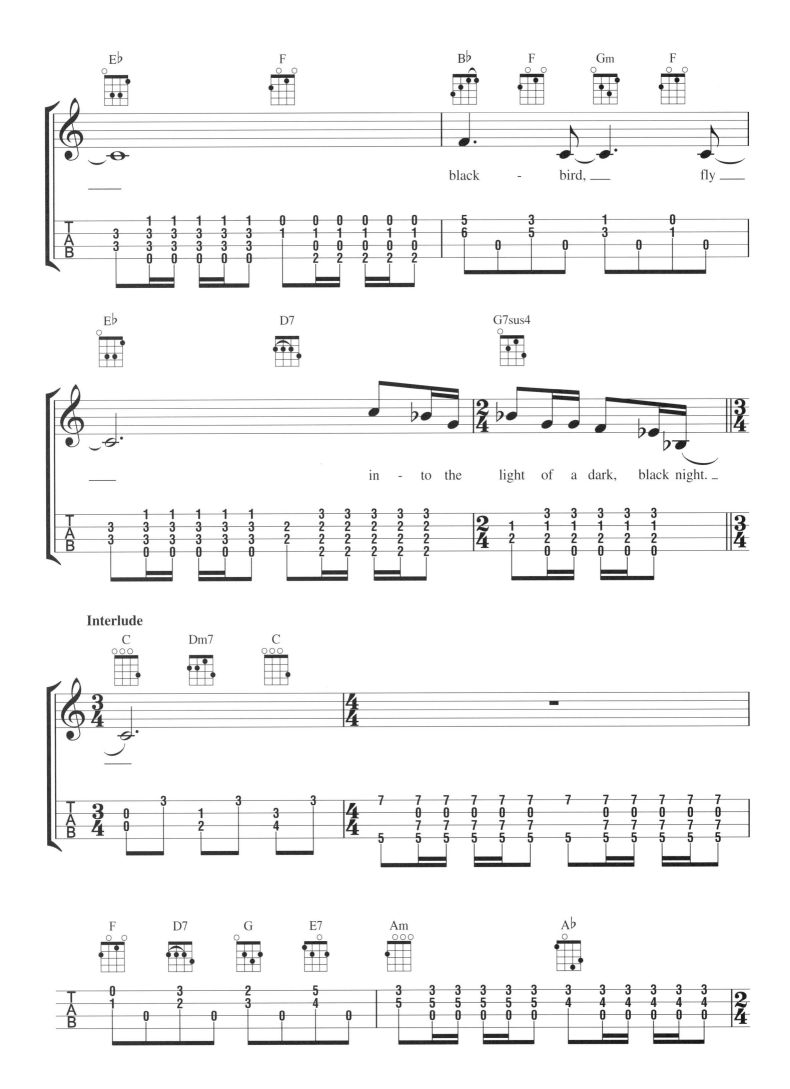

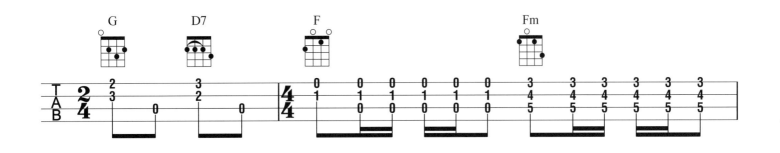

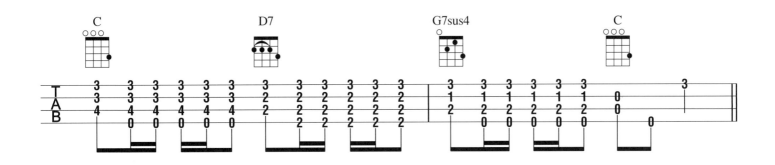

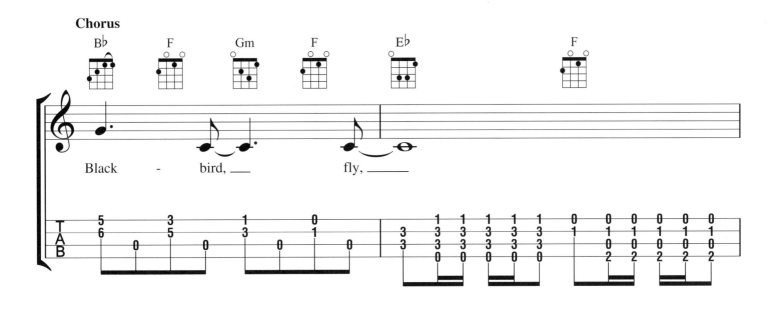

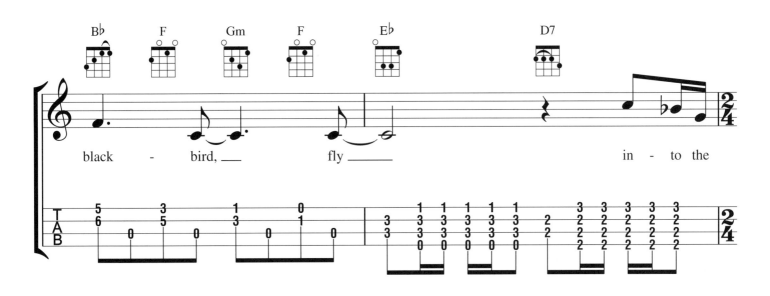

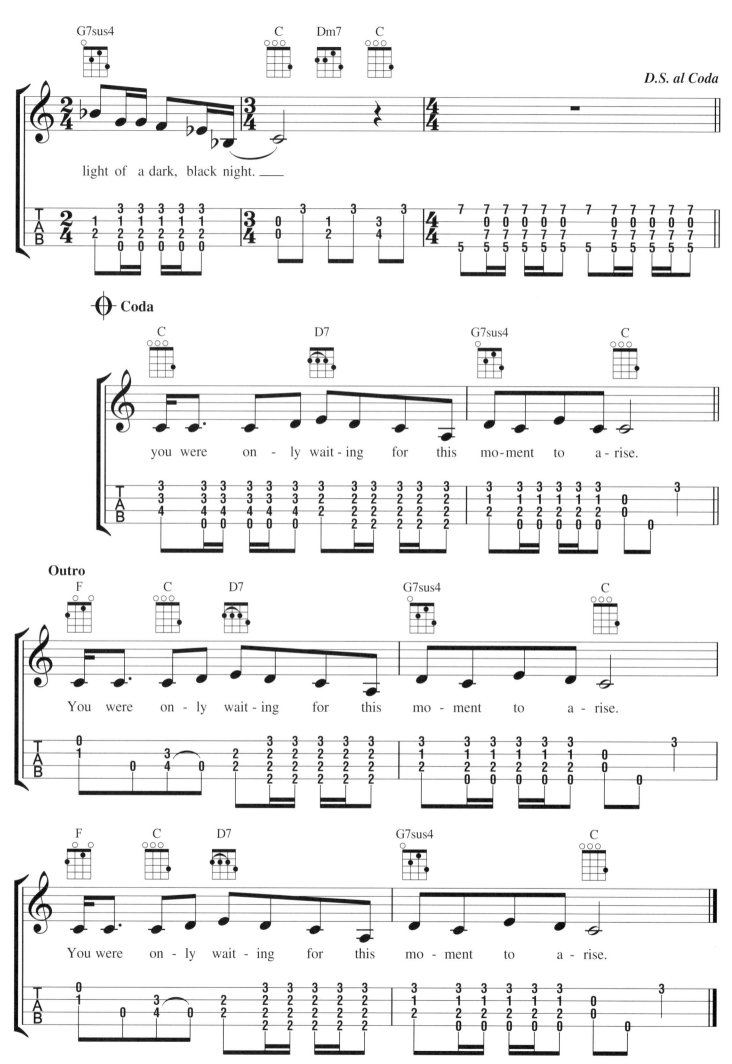

Come Together

Words and Music by John Lennon and Paul McCartney

First note

Verse
Moderately slow

1. Here come old flat-top, he come groov-in' up slow-ly. He got

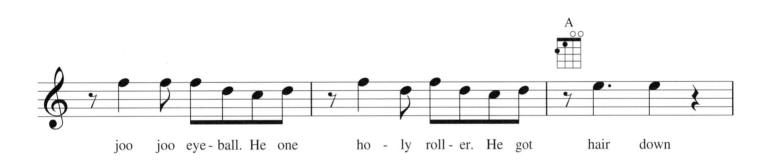

joo joo eye-ball. He one ho-ly roll-er. He got hair down

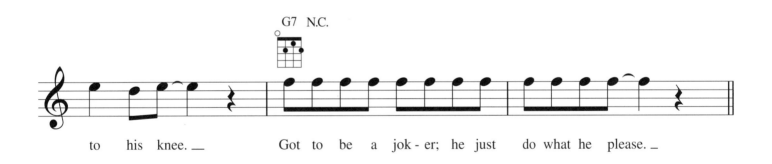

to his knee. __ Got to be a jok-er; he just do what he please. __

Interlude

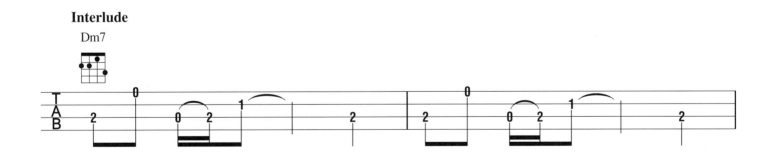

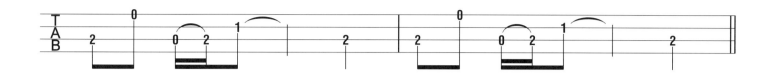

Verse

Dm7

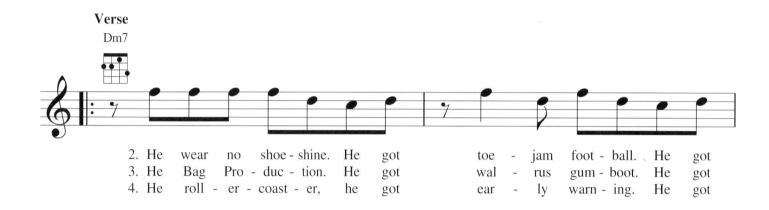

2. He wear no shoe-shine. He got   toe - jam foot - ball. He got
3. He Bag Pro - duc - tion. He got   wal - rus gum - boot. He got
4. He roll - er - coast - er, he got   ear - ly warn - ing. He got

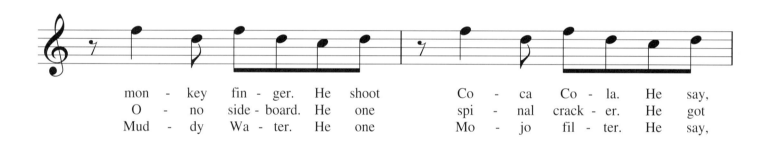

mon - key fin - ger. He shoot   Co - ca Co - la. He say,
O - no side - board. He one   spi - nal crack - er. He got
Mud - dy Wa - ter. He one   Mo - jo fil - ter. He say,

A

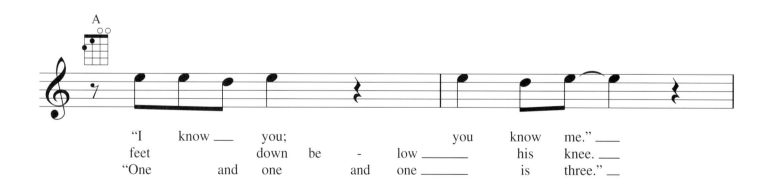

"I know ___ you;   you know me." ___
feet   down be - low _____ his knee. ___
"One   and one   and one _____ is three." ___

One thing I can tell you is you got to be free. \
Hold you in his arm-chair, you can feel his dis - ease. \
Got to be good-look-ing 'cause he so hard to see. \
Come to - geth -

Chorus

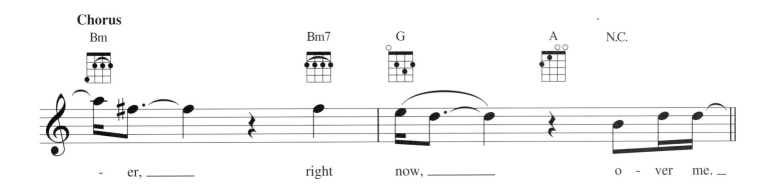

- er, _____ right now, _____ o - ver me. _

Interlude

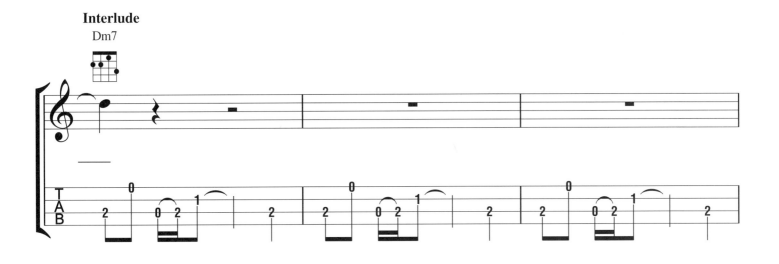

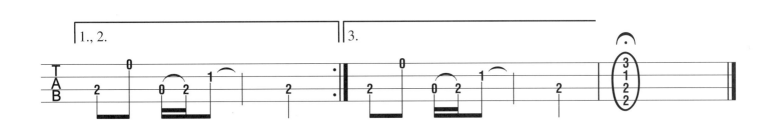

Day Tripper

Words and Music by John Lennon and Paul McCartney

First note

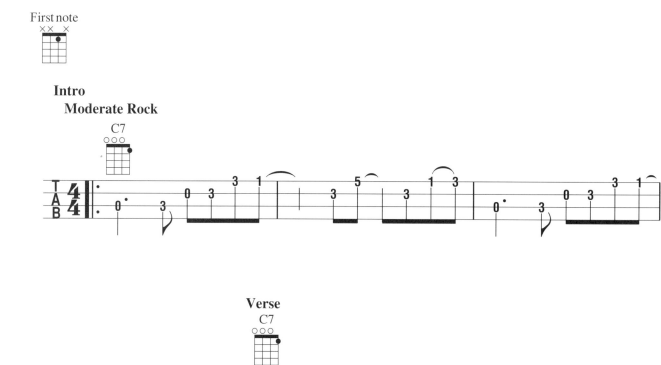

1. Got a good rea - son
2. She's a big teas - er,
3. Tried _ to please _ her,

for

tak - ing the eas - y way out. _____
she took me half ___ the way there. ___
she on - ly played _ one - night stands. _

Got a good rea - son
She's a big teas - er,
Tried _ to please _ her,

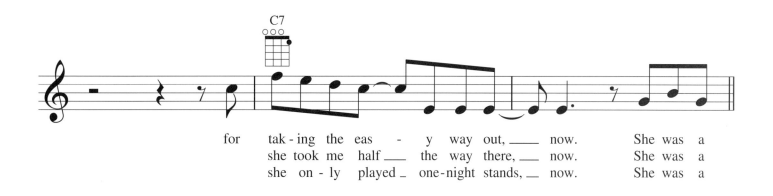

for   tak - ing   the   eas   -   y   way   out, ____   now.   She   was   a
she   took   me   half ____   the   way   there, ____   now.   She   was   a
she   on - ly   played ___   one-night   stands, ___   now.   She   was   a

Chorus

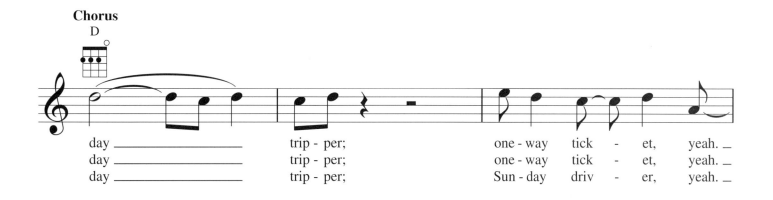

day _____   trip - per;   one - way   tick - et,   yeah. _
day _____   trip - per;   one - way   tick - et,   yeah. _
day _____   trip - per;   Sun - day   driv - er,   yeah. _

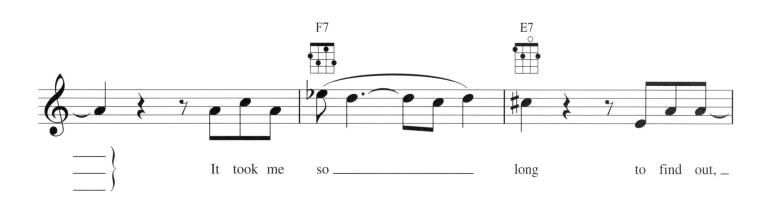

It   took   me   so _____   long   to   find   out, _

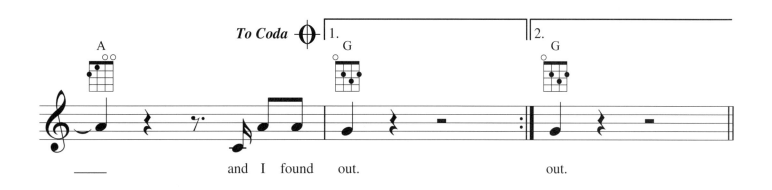

_____   and   I   found   out.   out.

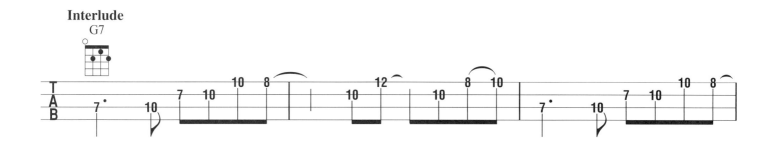

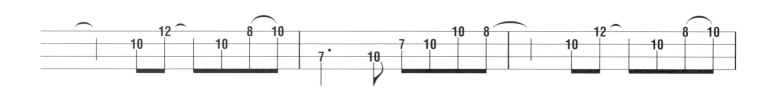

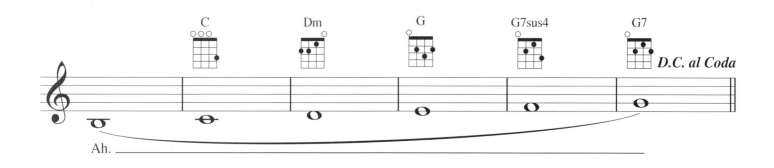

Ah. _____

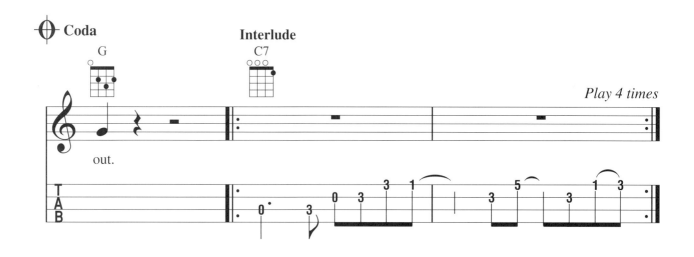

Coda

Interlude

Play 4 times

out.

Outro

Repeat and fade

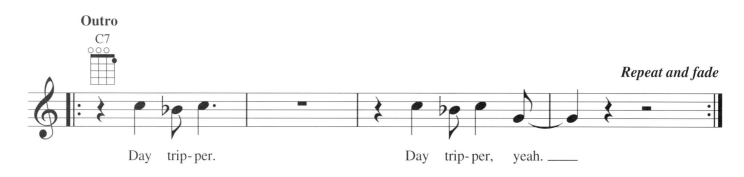

Day trip-per.   Day trip-per, yeah. ____

The Fool on the Hill

Words and Music by John Lennon and Paul McCartney

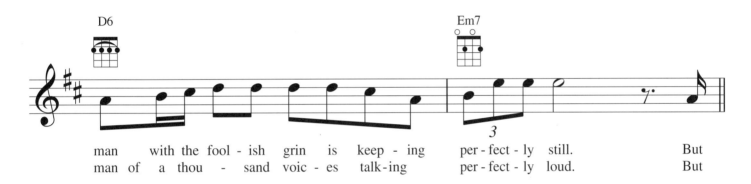

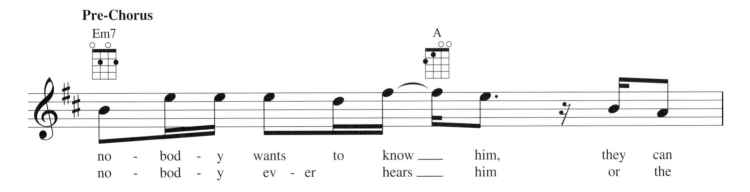

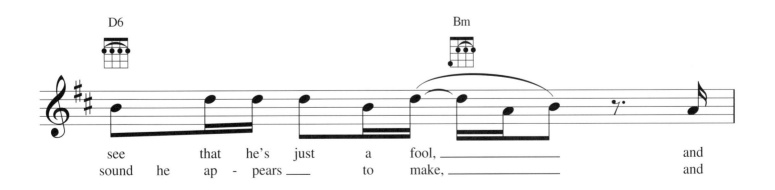

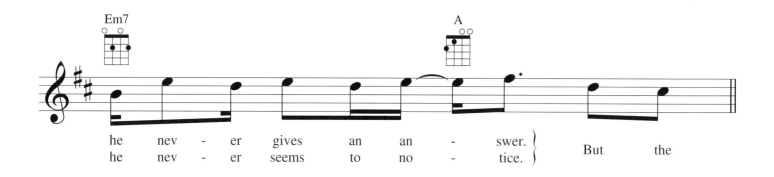

he nev - er gives an an - swer.
he nev - er seems to no - tice. } But the

Chorus

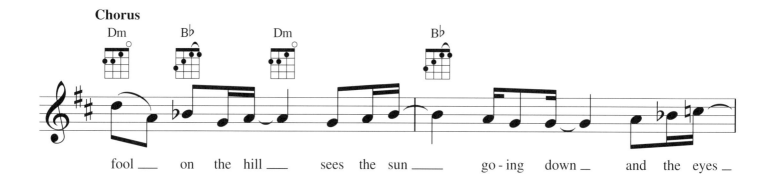

fool ___ on the hill ___ sees the sun ___ go - ing down ___ and the eyes ___

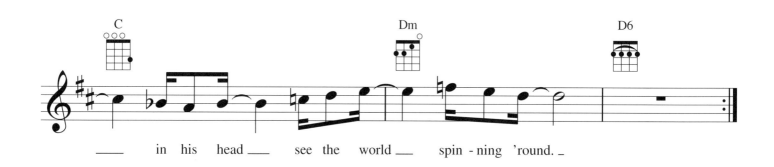

___ in his head ___ see the world ___ spin - ning 'round. ___

Recorder Solo

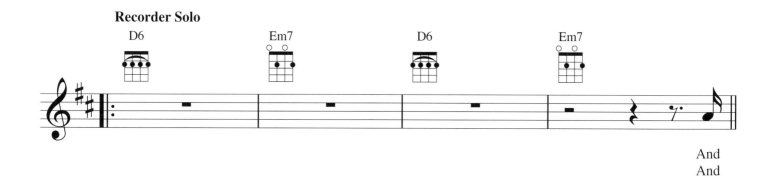

And
And

Pre-Chorus

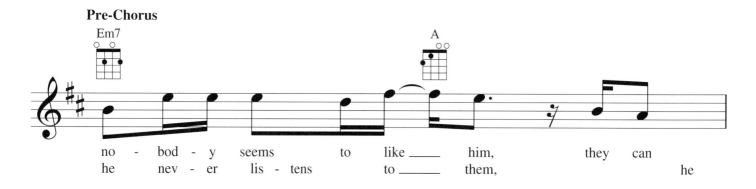

no - bod - y seems to like ___ him, they can
he nev - er lis - tens to ___ them, he

tell what he wants to do, _____ and
knows that they're __ the fools. _____

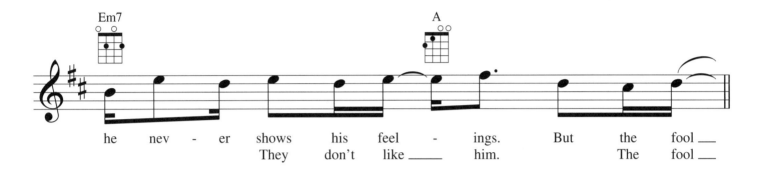

he nev - er shows his feel - ings. But the fool __
They don't like _____ him. The fool __

Chorus

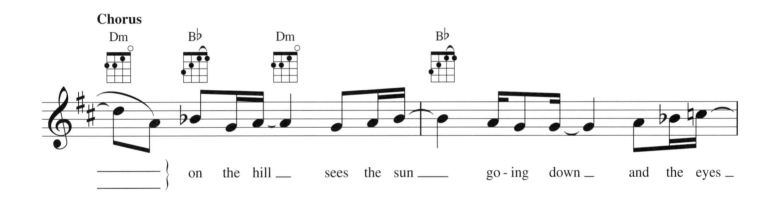

_____ } on the hill __ sees the sun _____ go - ing down __ and the eyes __

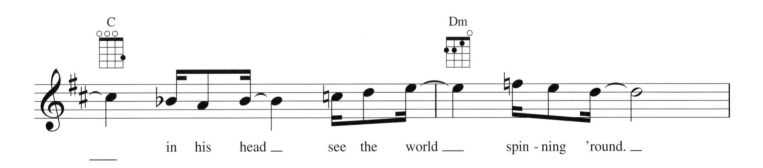

__ in his head __ see the world _____ spin - ning 'round. __

Outro   *Repeat and fade*

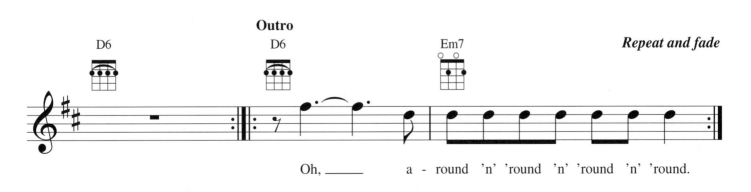

Oh, _____ a - round 'n' 'round 'n' 'round 'n' 'round.

Do You Want to Know a Secret?

Words and Music by John Lennon and Paul McCartney

First note

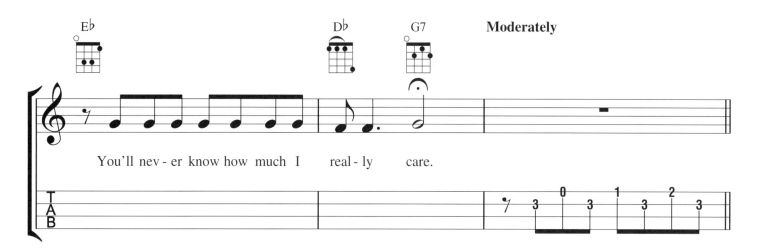

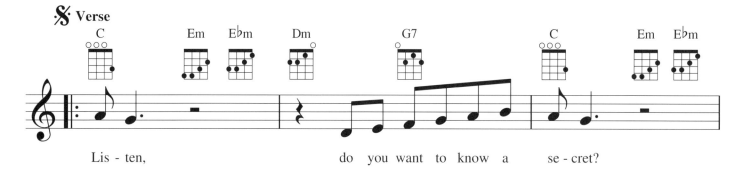

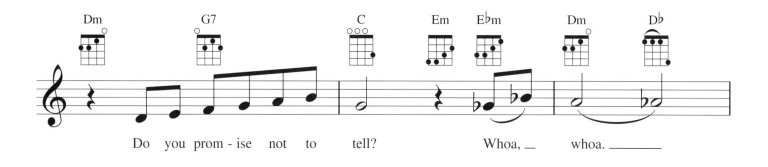

Eleanor Rigby

Words and Music by John Lennon and Paul McCartney

Additional Lyrics

2. Father McKenzie writing the words of a sermon that no one will hear,
No one comes near.
Look at him working, darning his socks in the night when there's nobody there,
What does he care?

3. Eleanor Rigby died in the church and was buried along with her name,
Nobody came.
Father McKenzie wiping the dirt from his hands as he walks from the grave,
No one was saved.

Golden Slumbers

Words and Music by John Lennon and Paul McCartney

Good Night

Words and Music by John Lennon and Paul McCartney

Now the moon be-gins to shine; / Now the sun turns out his light; / good night, sleep tight.

Dream sweet dreams for me. Dream sweet dreams for

you. Mm, _____ mm, _____

To Coda ✛ **Interlude**

D.S. al Coda ✛ **Coda**

mm. _____

Slower

(Whispered:) Good night, good night, ev - 'ry - bod - y,

ev - 'ry - bod - y, ev - 'ry - where, good night.

I Saw Her Standing There

Words and Music by John Lennon and Paul McCartney

Chorus

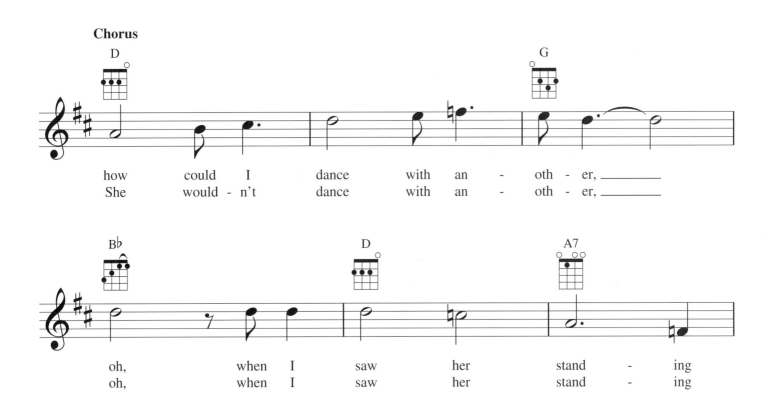

how could I dance with an - oth - er, _____
She would - n't dance with an - oth - er, _____

oh, when I saw her stand - ing
oh, when I saw her stand - ing

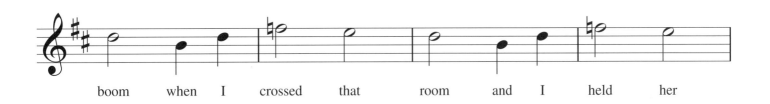

Bridge

there? 2. Well,
there. Well, my heart went

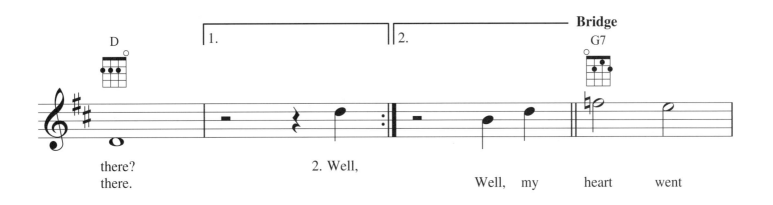

boom when I crossed that room and I held her

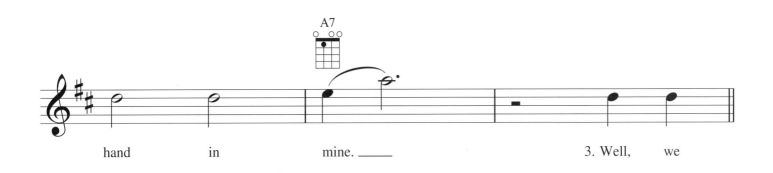

hand in mine. _____ 3. Well, we

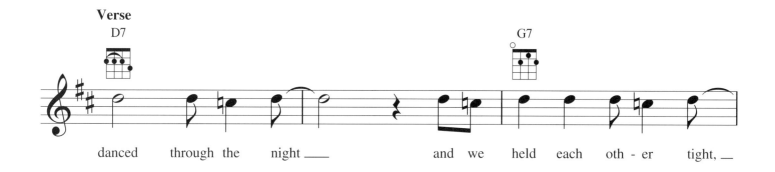

Verse

danced   through the   night ___   and we held each oth - er   tight, ___

___   and be - fore too long, ___   I   fell   in   love   with

Chorus

her. _____   Now,   I'll   nev - er

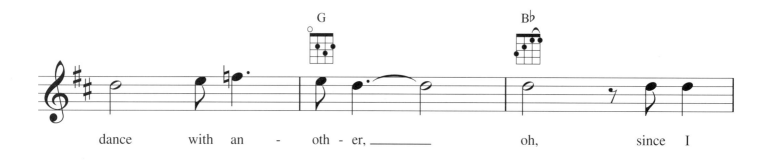

dance   with an - oth - er, _____   oh,   since   I

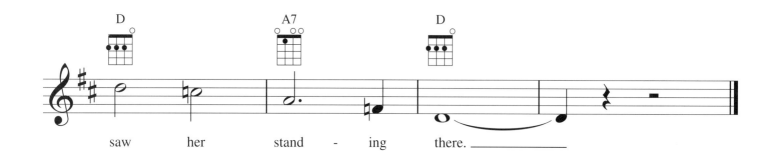

saw   her   stand - ing   there. _____

Hello, Goodbye

Words and Music by John Lennon and Paul McCartney

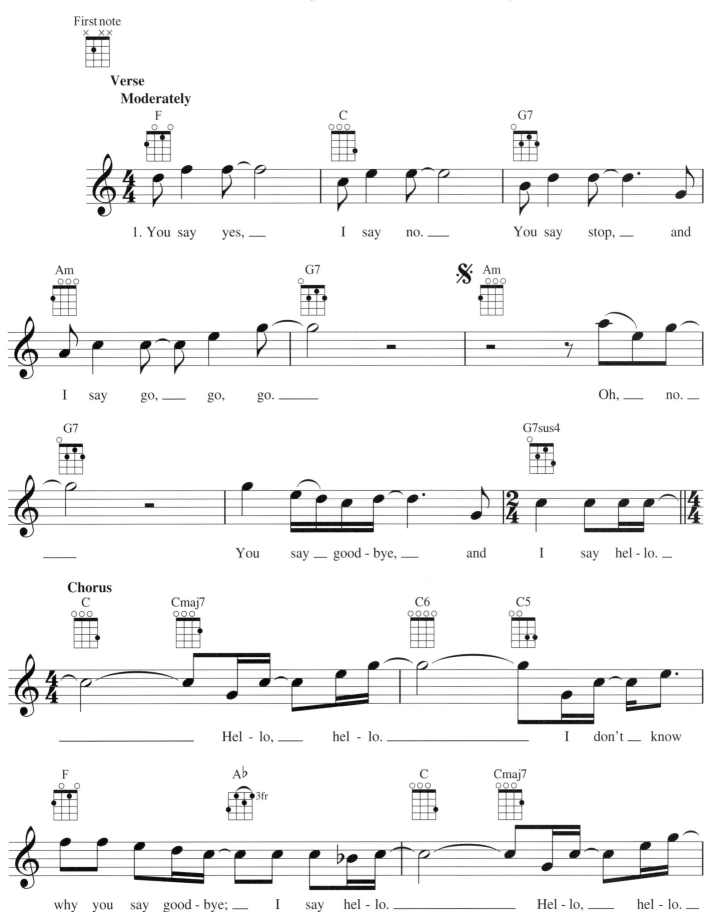

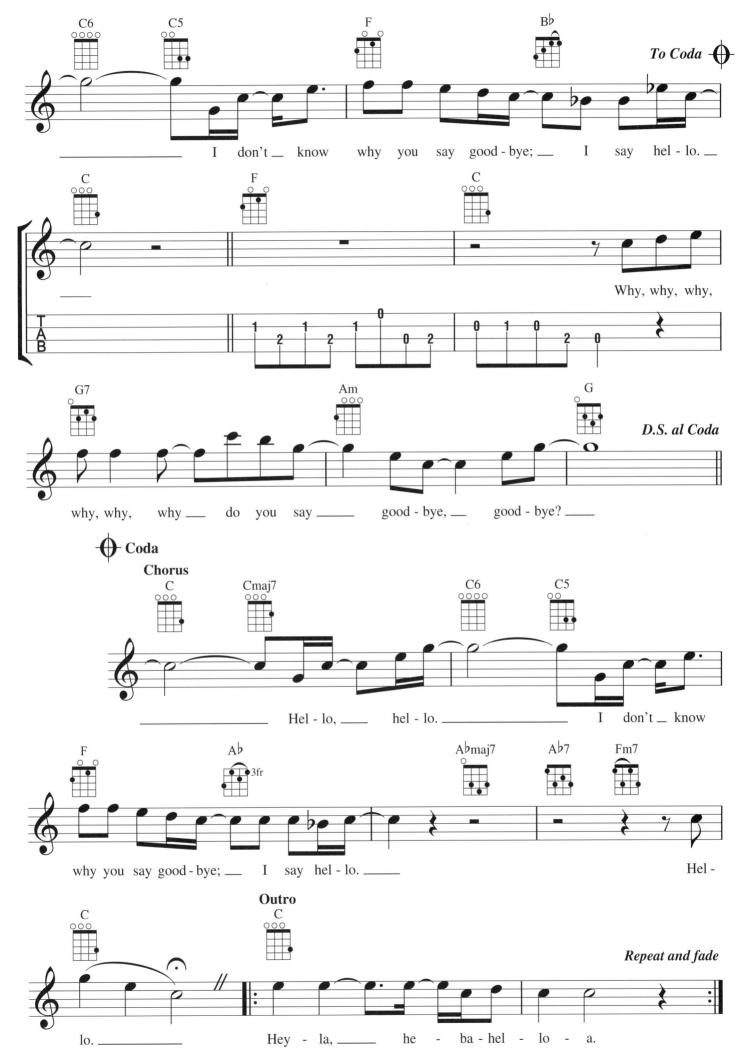

If I Fell

Words and Music by John Lennon and Paul McCartney

First note

Intro
Moderately

If I fell in love with you, would you prom - ise to be true and

help me un - der - stand? __ 'Cause I've been in love be - fore, and I

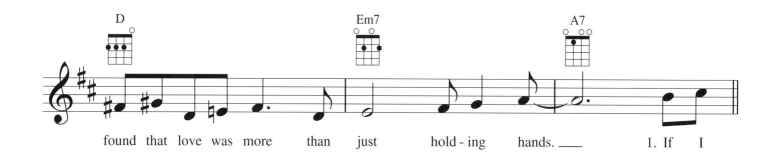

found that love was more than just hold - ing hands. __ 1. If I

Verse

give my heart to you, I must be sure from the
(2.) trust in you, oh, please don't run and hide. If I

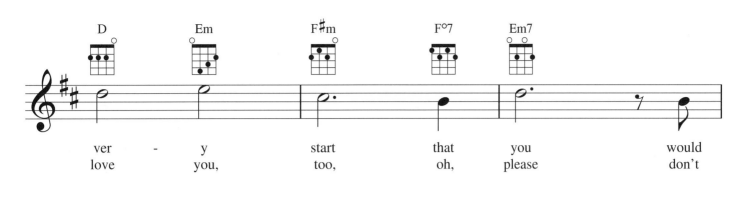

ver - y   start   that   you   would
love   you,   too,   oh,   please   don't

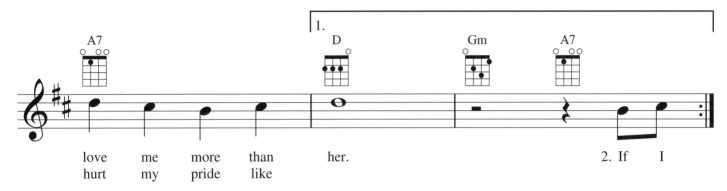

love   me   more   than   her.   2. If   I
hurt   my   pride   like

Bridge

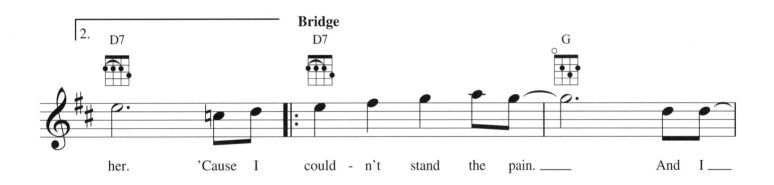

her.   'Cause   I   could - n't   stand   the   pain. _____   And   I ___

_____   would   be   sad   if   our   new   love   was   in

Verse

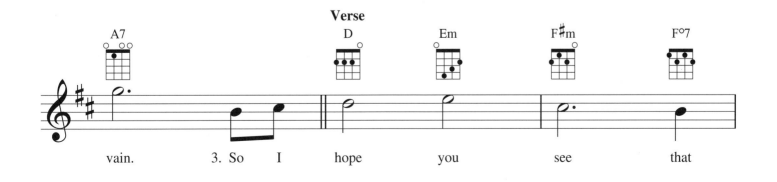

vain.   3. So   I   hope   you   see   that

I Will

Words and Music by John Lennon and Paul McCartney

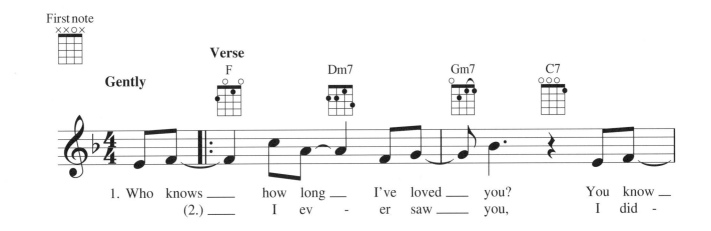

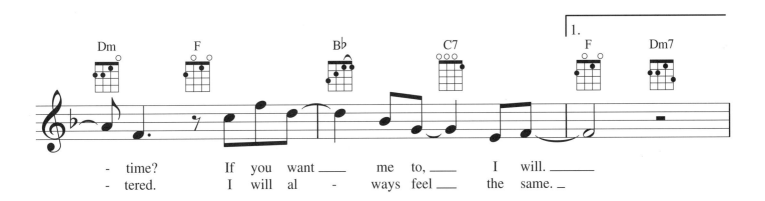

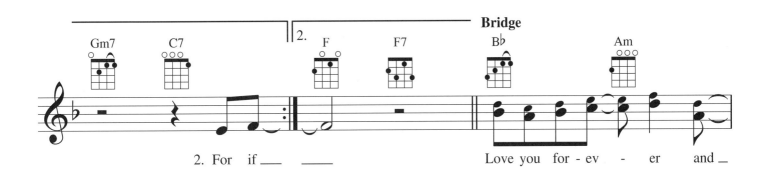

_____ for - ev - er. Love you with all _____ my heart. _____

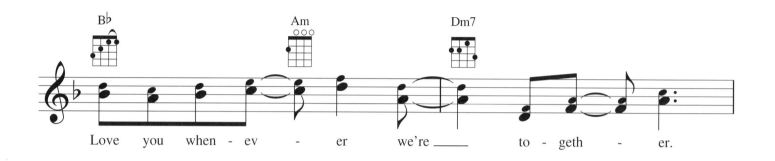

Love you when - ev - er we're _____ to - geth - er.

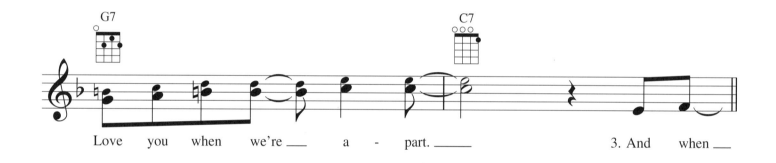

Love you when we're _____ a - part. _____ 3. And when _____

Verse

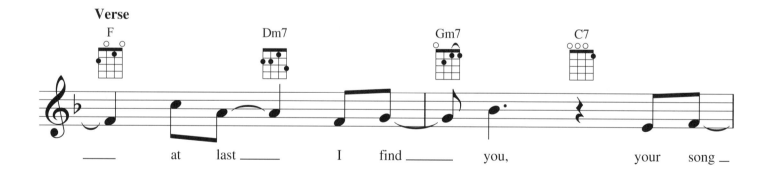

_____ at last _____ I find _____ you, your song _____

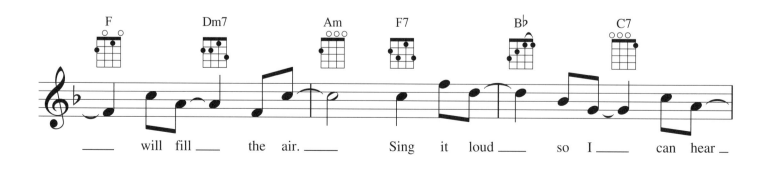

_____ will fill _____ the air. _____ Sing it loud _____ so I _____ can hear _____

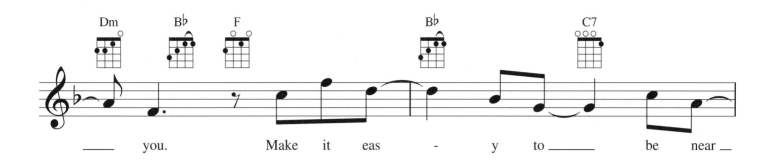

_____ you. Make it eas - y to _____ be near _____

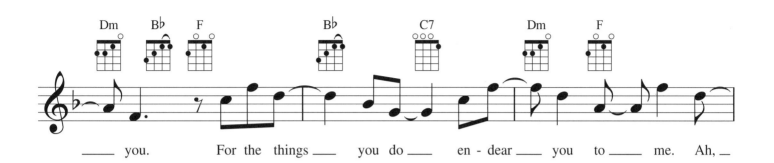

_____ you. For the things _____ you do _____ en - dear _____ you to _____ me. Ah, _____

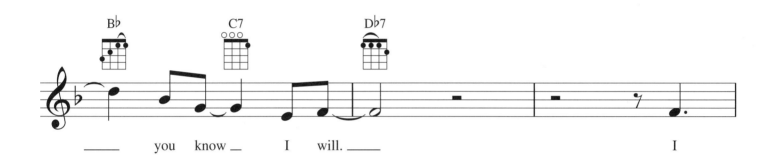

_____ you know _ I will. _____ I

Outro

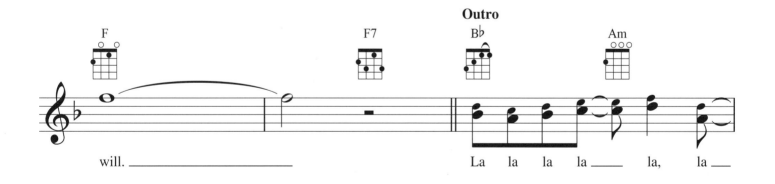

will. _____ La la la la _____ la, la _____

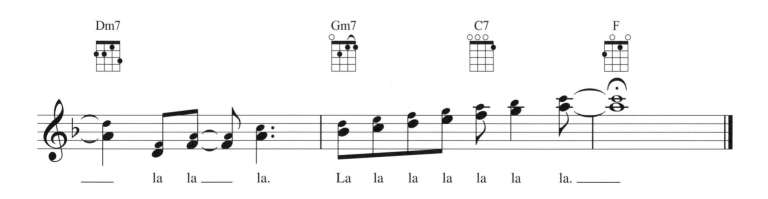

_____ la la _____ la. La la la la la la la. _____

Lady Madonna

Words and Music by John Lennon and Paul McCartney

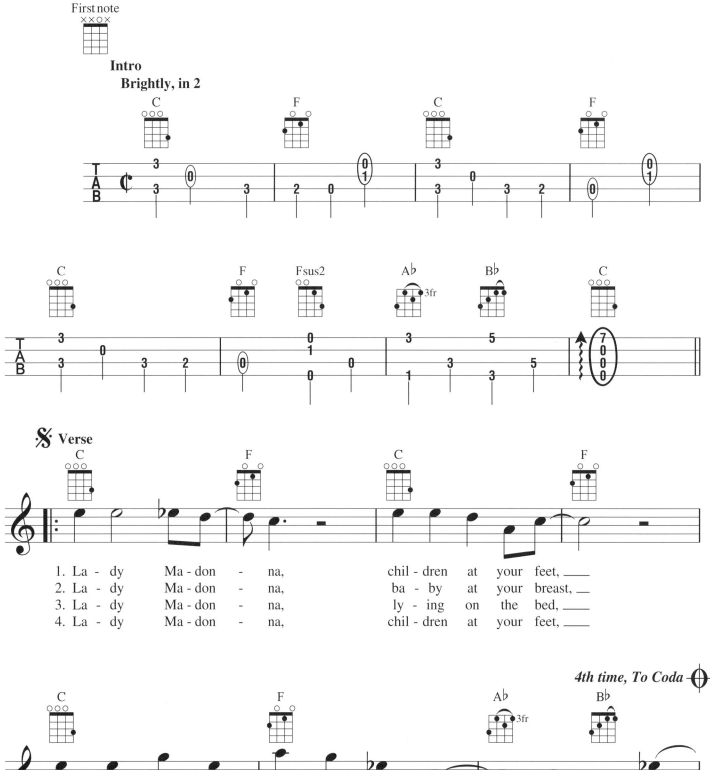

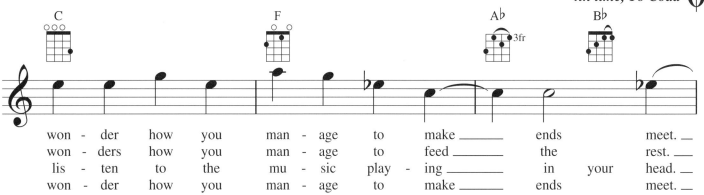

Who finds the mon - ey
Instrumental
Instrumental

when you pay the rent? _____ Did you think that

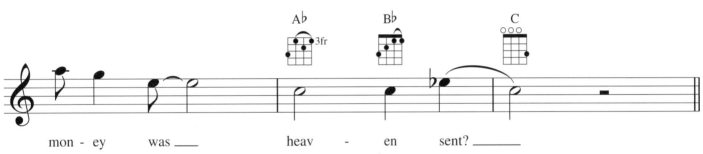

mon - ey was _____ heav - en sent? _____

Bridge

Fri - day night _____ ar - rives _____ with - out _____ a suit - case. _____
Instrumental
Tues - day af - ter - noon _____ is nev - er end - ing. _____

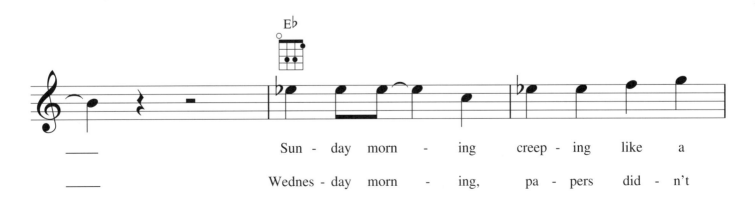

_____ Sun - day morn - ing creep - ing like a
_____ Wednes - day morn - ing, pa - pers did - n't

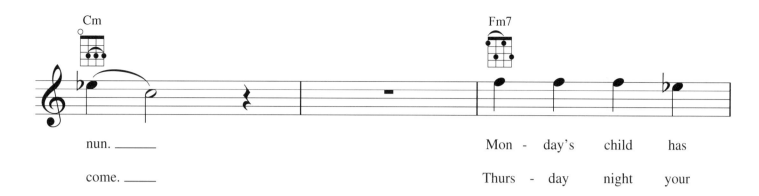

nun. _____

Mon - day's child has

come. _____

Thurs - day night your

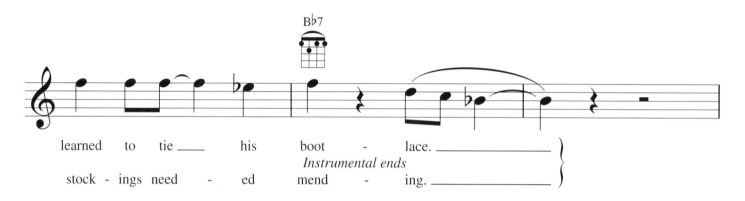

learned to tie _____ his boot - lace. _____

Instrumental ends

stock - ings need - ed mend - ing. _____

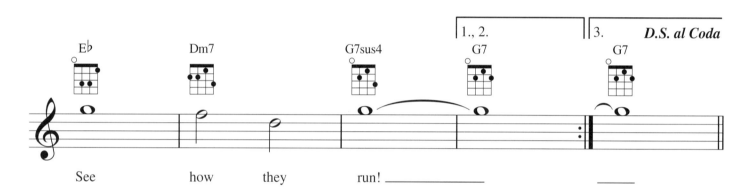

See how they run! _____

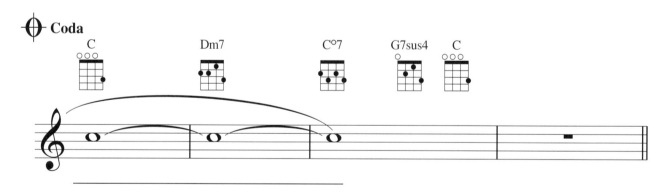

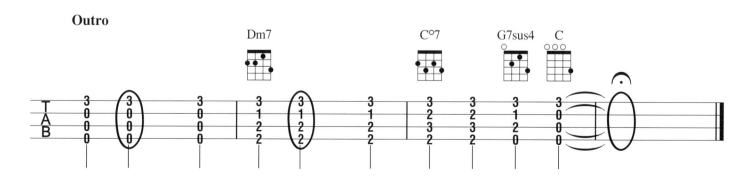

Revolution

Words and Music by John Lennon and Paul McCartney

world.
plan.
head.

You tell me that it's e-vo-lu-
You ask me for a con-tri-bu-
You tell me it's the in-sti-tu-

-tion, _____ well, _____ you know, _____ we all want _
-tion, _____ well, _____ you know, _____ we're all do-
-tion, _____ well, _____ you know, _____ you bet-ter free _

_____ to change the world. _____
-ing what we can. _____
_____ your mind in - stead. _____

But when you talk a - bout de - struc - tion, _____
But if you want mon-ey for peo-ple with minds that hate, _____
But if you go car - ry - ing pic-tures of Chair - man Mao, _____

don't you know that you can count me out. __ }
all I can tell you is, "Broth-er, you have to wait." __ }
you ain't go - ing to make it with an - y - one an - y - how. __ }

Chorus

Don't you know it's gon-na be _____ al - right, _

The Long and Winding Road

Words and Music by John Lennon and Paul McCartney

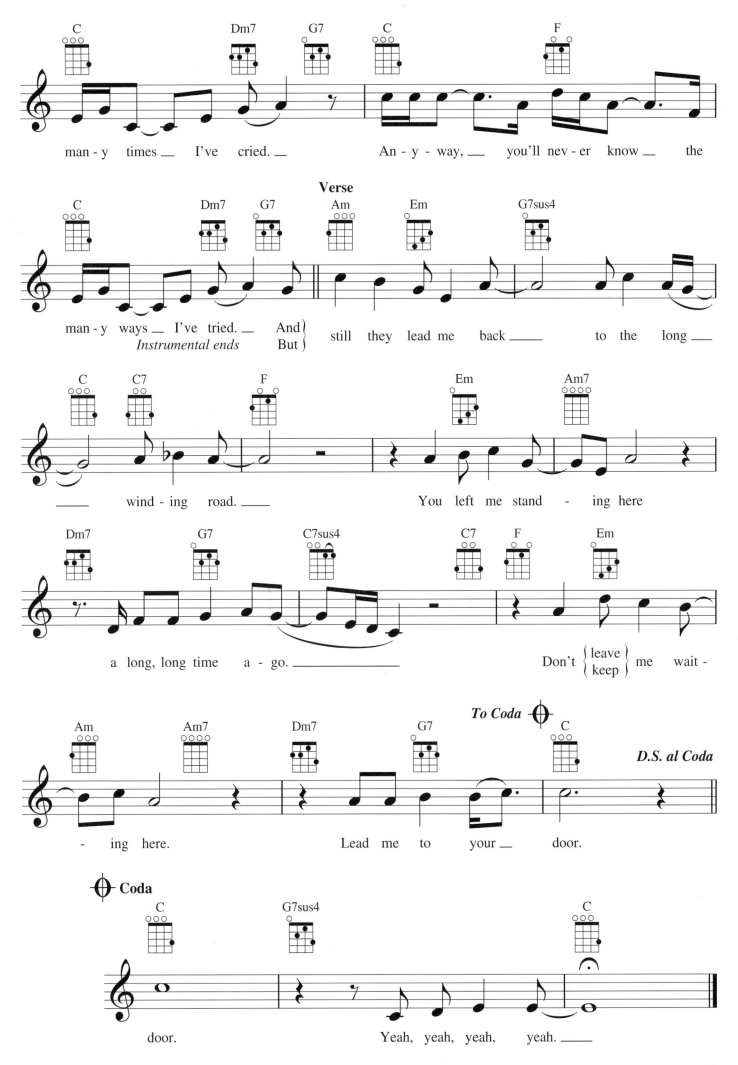

man - y times ___ I've cried. ___ An - y - way, ___ you'll nev - er know ___ the

Verse

man - y ways ___ I've tried. ___ And / But \ still they lead me back _____ to the long ___
Instrumental ends

_____ wind - ing road. ___ You left me stand - ing here

a long, long time a - go. _____ Don't { leave / keep } me wait -

To Coda ⊕
D.S. al Coda

- ing here. Lead me to your ___ door.

⊕ **Coda**

door. Yeah, yeah, yeah, yeah. ___

Norwegian Wood
(This Bird Has Flown)

Words and Music by John Lennon and Paul McCartney

First note

1. I once had a girl, ____ or should I say, she once had
2. *Instrumental*

me. She showed me her room, is-n't it good Nor-we-gian

wood? She asked me to stay and she told me to sit an-y-where.
End instrumental She told me she worked in the morn-ing and start-ed to laugh. ___

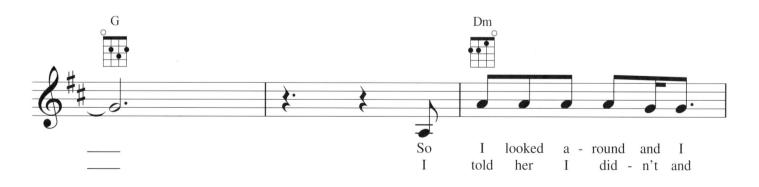

____ So I looked a-round and I
____ I told her I did-n't and

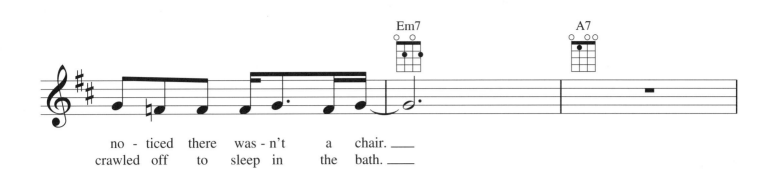

no - ticed there was - n't a chair. ____
crawled off to sleep in the bath. ____

Verse

2. I sat on a rug, bid-ing my time, drink-ing her wine.
4. And when I a - woke, I was a - lone; this bird had flown.

We talked un - til two, and then she said, "It's time for bed." _
So, I lit a fire, is - n't it

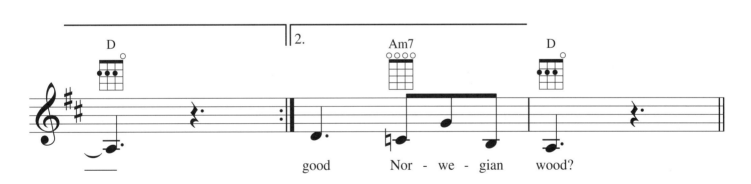

good Nor - we - gian wood?

Outro

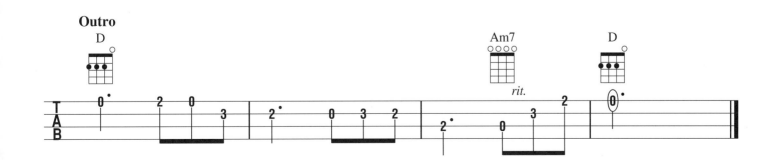

She Loves You

Words and Music by John Lennon and Paul McCartney

Pre-Chorus

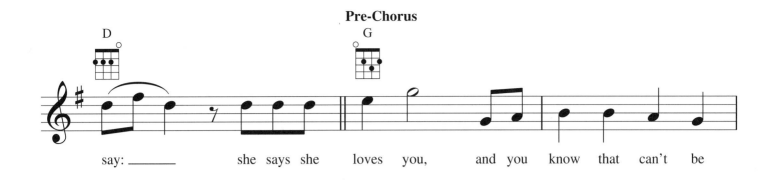

say: _____ she says she loves you, and you know that can't be

bad. Yes, she loves you, and you

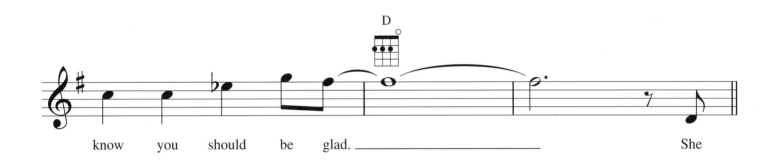

know you should be glad. _____ She

Verse

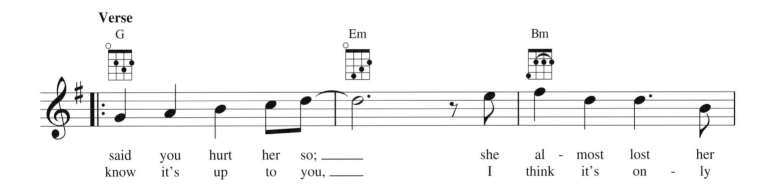

said you hurt her so; _____ she al - most lost her
know it's up to you, _____ I think it's on - ly

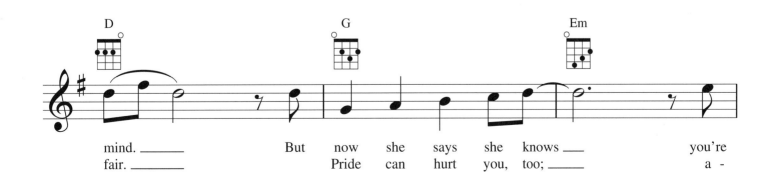

mind. _____ But now she says she knows ___ you're
fair. _____ Pride can hurt you, too; _____ a -

not the hurt - ing kind. _____ She says she loves you, and you
pol - o - gize to her. _____ Be - cause she loves you, and you

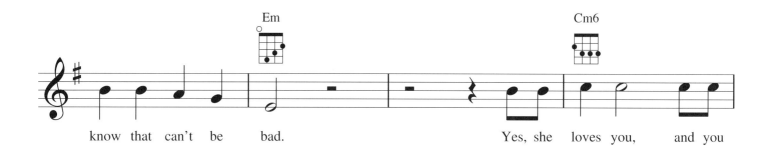

know that can't be bad. Yes, she loves you, and you

Chorus

know you should be glad. _____ Ooh! ___ She loves you, yeah,

yeah, yeah. _ She loves you, yeah, yeah, yeah. _ And with a

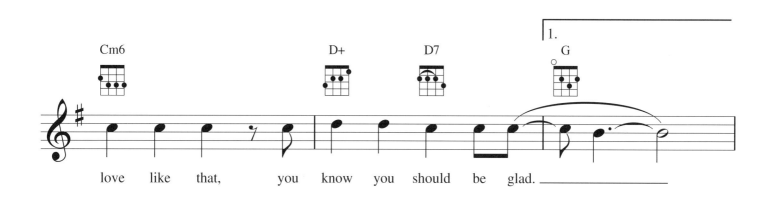

love like that, you know you should be glad. _____

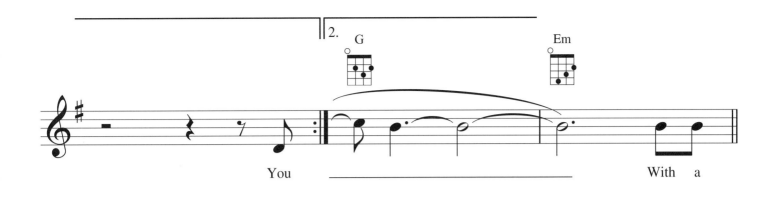

2.

You _____ With a

Outro

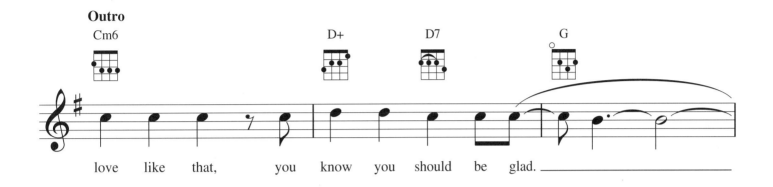

love like that, you know you should be glad. _____

_____ With a love like that, you know you should _____ be

glad. Yeah, yeah, yeah, _____ yeah,

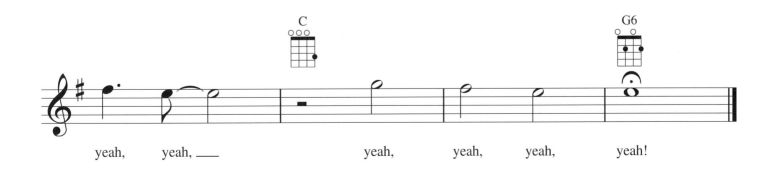

yeah, yeah, _____ yeah, yeah, yeah, yeah!

Something

Words and Music by George Harrison

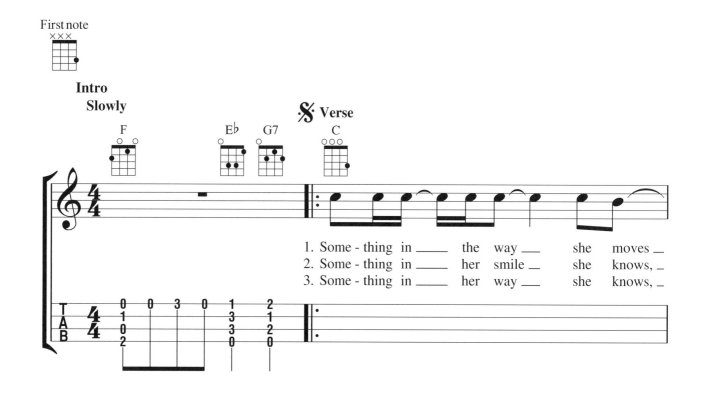

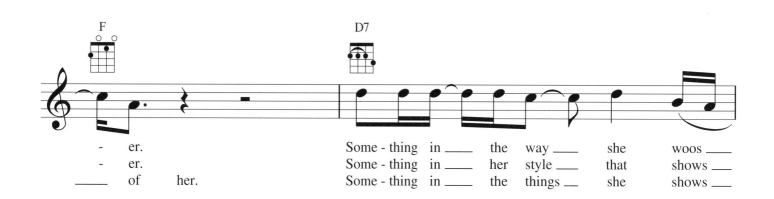

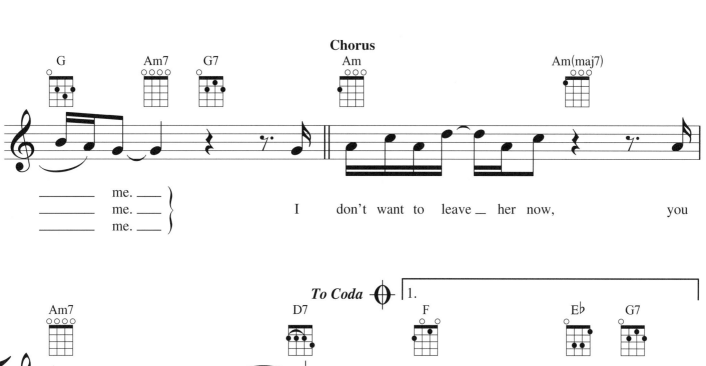

Chorus

_____ me. _____
_____ me. _____
_____ me. _____

I don't want to leave __ her now,   you

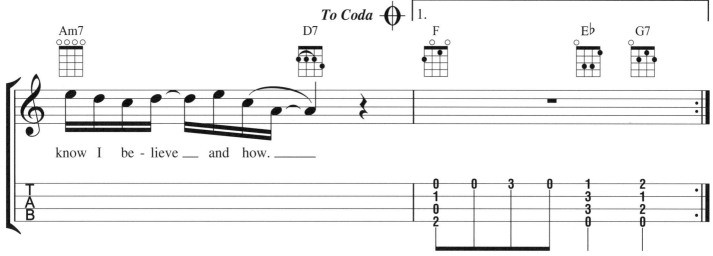

To Coda ⊕ | 1.

know I be - lieve __ and how. _____

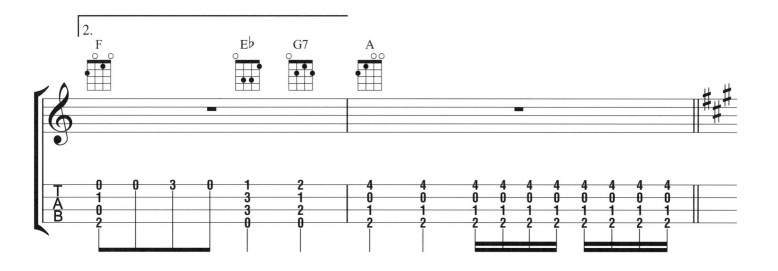

2.

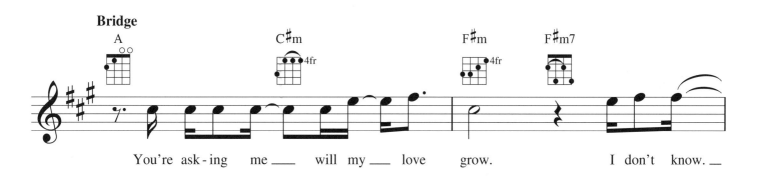

Bridge

You're ask - ing me __ will my __ love grow.   I don't know. __

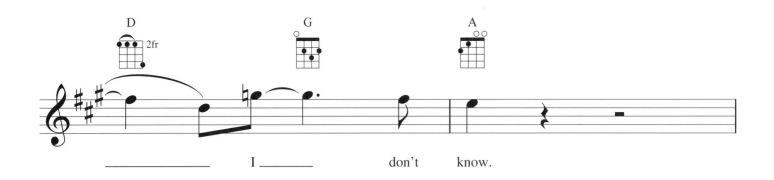

_____ I _____ don't know.

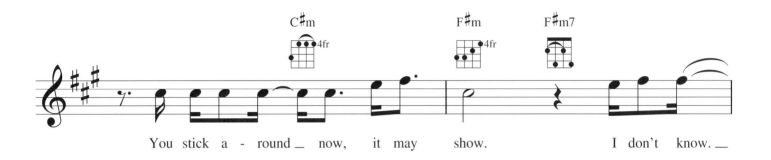

You stick a - round __ now, it may show. I don't know. __

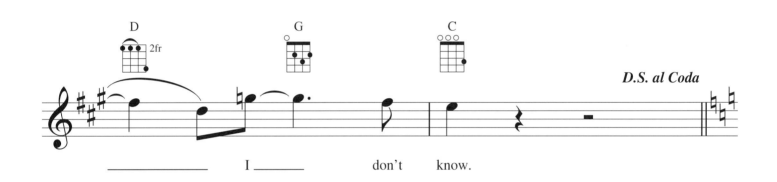

D.S. al Coda

_____ I _____ don't know.

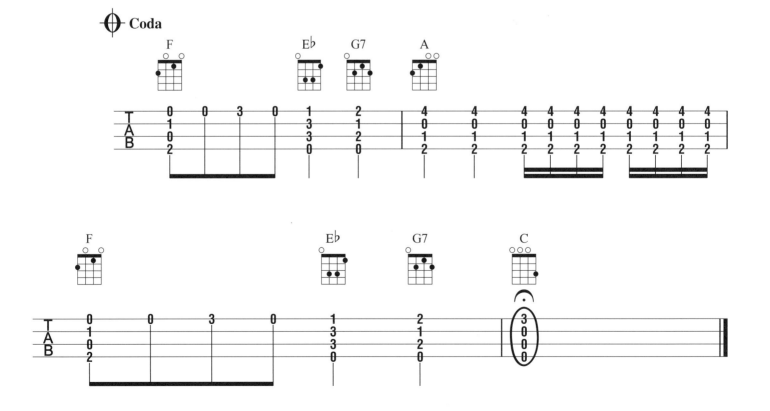

Coda

When I'm Sixty-Four

Words and Music by John Lennon and Paul McCartney

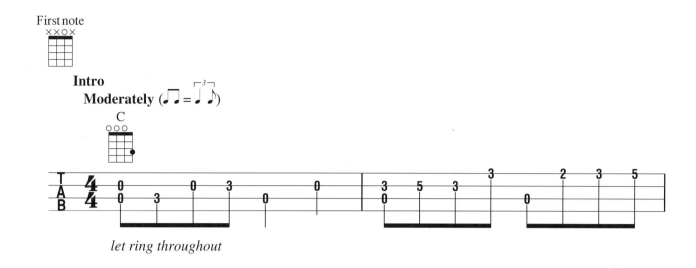

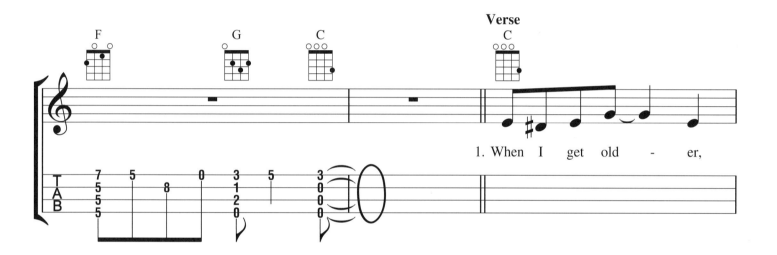

bot - tle of wine? __ If I'd been out __ till quar - ter to three, __

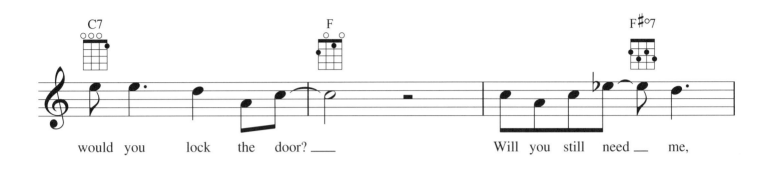

would you lock the door? ___ Will you still need __ me,

will you still feed ___ me when I'm six - ty - four?

Bridge

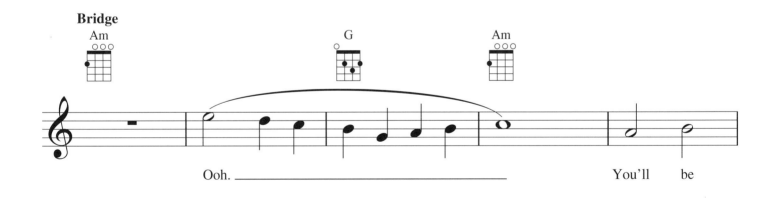

Ooh. _____ You'll be

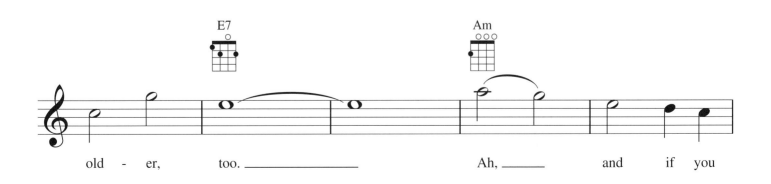

old - er, too. _____ Ah, _____ and if you

say   the   word, _____   I   could   stay   with

you.

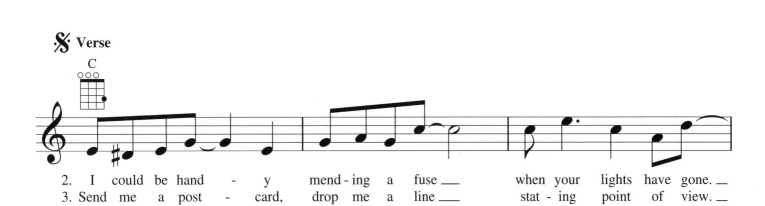

%. Verse

2. I could be hand - y   mend - ing   a   fuse ___   when your   lights   have gone. __
3. Send me a post - card,   drop me   a   line ___   stat - ing   point   of   view. __

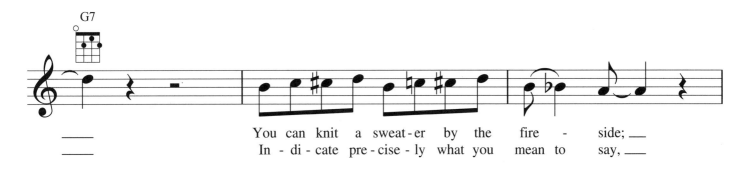

___   You can knit a sweat-er by the   fire - side; __
___   In - di - cate pre - cise - ly what you   mean to   say, __

Sun - day   morn - ing,   go   for   a   ride. __   Do - ing   the gar - den,
yours   sin - cere - ly   wast - ing   a - way. __   Give me your an - swer,

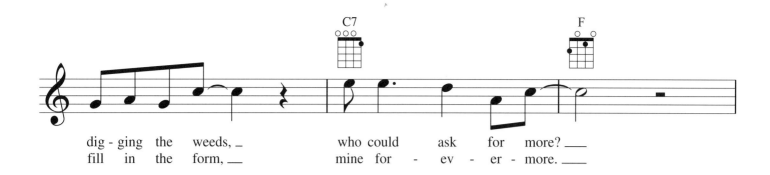

dig - ging the weeds, __ who could ask for more? __
fill in the form, __ mine for - ev - er - more. __

To Coda ⊕

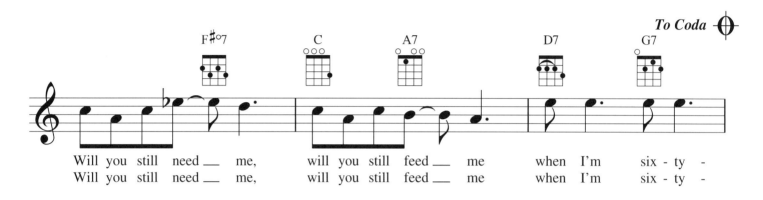

Will you still need __ me, will you still feed __ me when I'm six - ty -
Will you still need __ me, will you still feed __ me when I'm six - ty -

Bridge

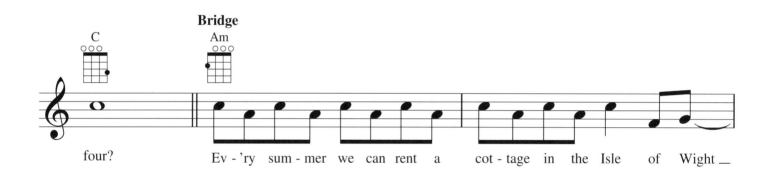

four? Ev - 'ry sum - mer we can rent a cot - tage in the Isle of Wight __

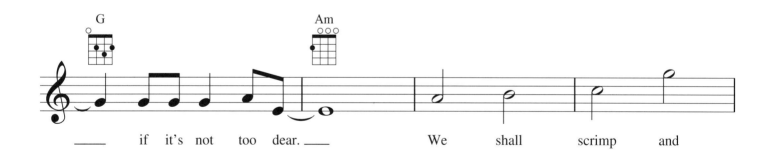

__ if it's not too dear. __ We shall scrimp and

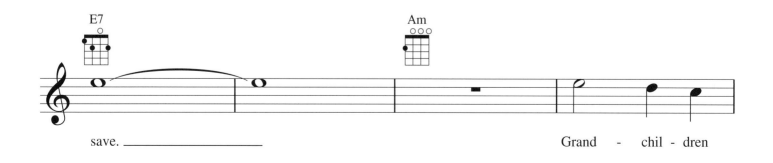

save. _____ Grand - chil - dren

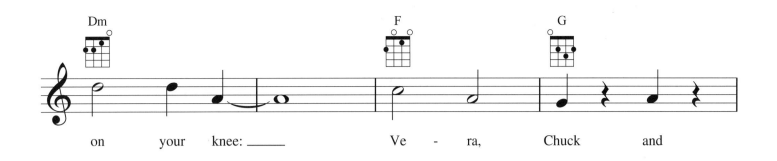

on your knee: _____ Ve - ra, Chuck and

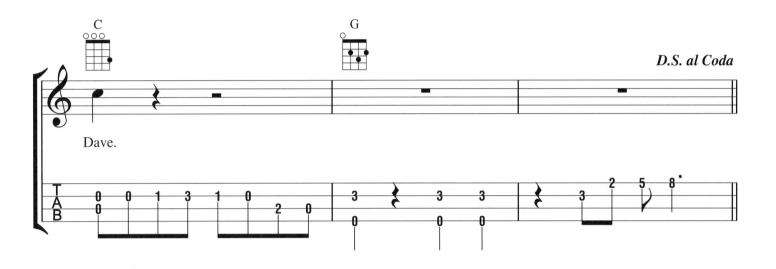

D.S. al Coda

Dave.

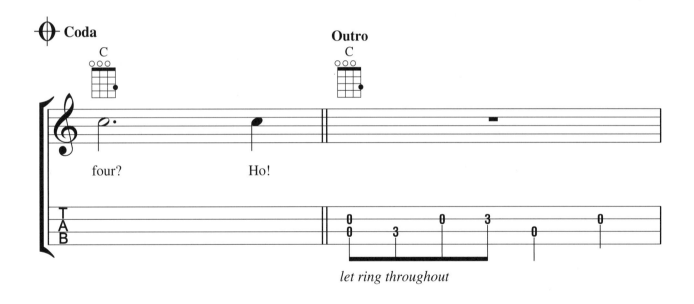

Coda

Outro

four? Ho!

let ring throughout

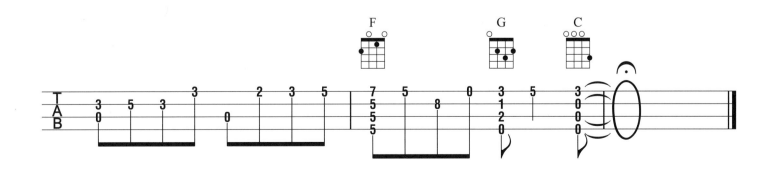

With a Little Help from My Friends

Words and Music by John Lennon and Paul McCartney

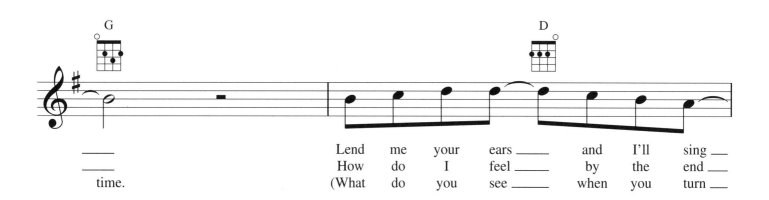

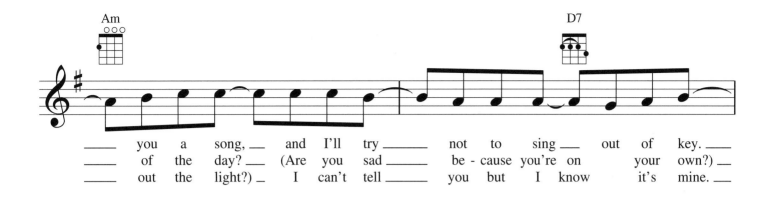

_____ you a song, ___ and I'll try _____ not to sing ___ out of key. _____
_____ of the day? ___ (Are you sad _____ be - cause you're on your own?) ___
_____ out the light?) ___ I can't tell _____ you but I know it's mine. ___

Chorus

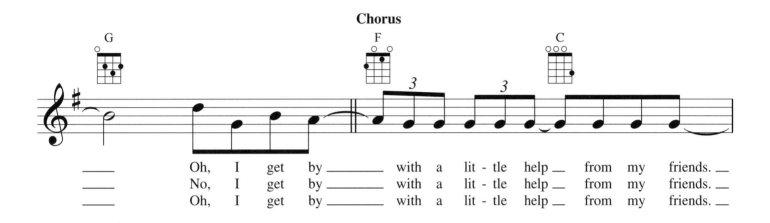

_____ Oh, I get by _____ with a lit - tle help ___ from my friends. ___
_____ No, I get by _____ with a lit - tle help ___ from my friends. ___
_____ Oh, I get by _____ with a lit - tle help ___ from my friends. ___

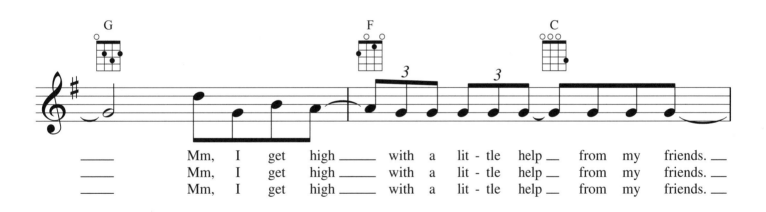

_____ Mm, I get high _____ with a lit - tle help ___ from my friends. ___
_____ Mm, I get high _____ with a lit - tle help ___ from my friends. ___
_____ Mm, I get high _____ with a lit - tle help ___ from my friends. ___

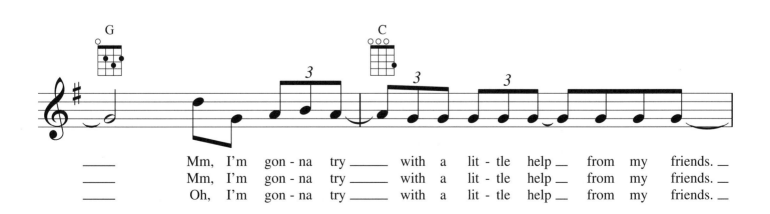

_____ Mm, I'm gon - na try _____ with a lit - tle help ___ from my friends. ___
_____ Mm, I'm gon - na try _____ with a lit - tle help ___ from my friends. ___
_____ Oh, I'm gon - na try _____ with a lit - tle help ___ from my friends. ___

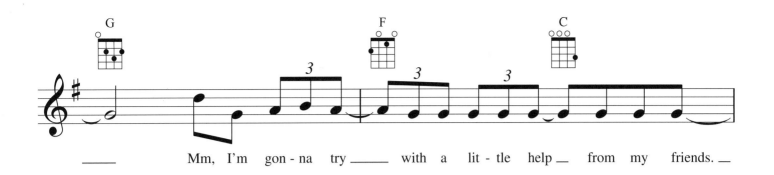

____ Mm, I'm gon - na try ____ with a lit - tle help ____ from my friends. ____

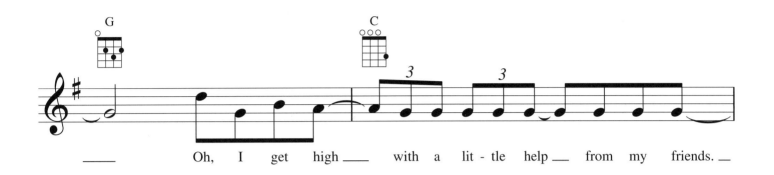

____ Oh, I get high ____ with a lit - tle help ____ from my friends. ____

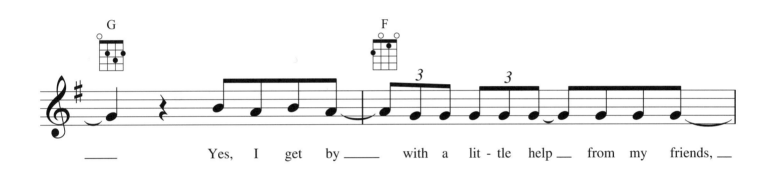

____ Yes, I get by ____ with a lit - tle help ____ from my friends, ____

____ with a lit - tle help ____ from my friends. ____

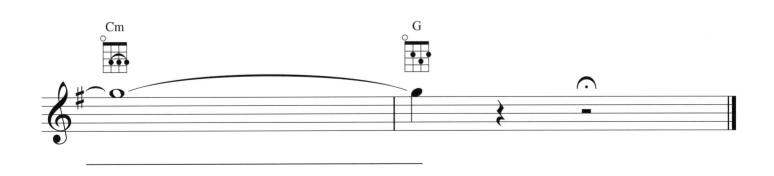